Grace at the KITCHEN TABLE

Prayers for Alignment in Work and Family Life

DIANA RILEY

Copyright © 2020 DIANA RILEY

All rights reserved. No part of this publication may be reproduced, distributed, or transmitted in any form or by any means, including photocopying, recording, or other electronic or mechanical methods, without prior written consent of the publisher, except in case of brief quotations embodied in reviews and certain other non-commercial uses permitted by the copyright law.

Contents

Let's Say Grace 1
    Daily Bread

Why Not You? 7
    Daily Bread

What's in Your Hands 15
    Daily Bread

Home is Where the Heart Is 23
    Daily Bread

A Wise Woman Builds 31
    Daily Bread

Mind Your Business 37
    Daily Bread

Plant Your Garden 43
    Daily Bread

It's Harvest Time 49
    Daily Bread

Grace Recipes 59

Let's Say Grace

Imagine standing in front of a judge for an unpaid speeding ticket and you have no excuses. The only real reason you have is you forgot and didn't prioritize paying it. You're a praying woman, so your hope, and trust is in God. You are out of chances and at the mercy of the judge. Because the effectual fervent prayer of the righteous avails much, the judge gives you an extended payment deadline, and you have been given another chance. Grace is a two-way street. Imagine your child just accidently broke your favorite vase. He pleaded with you and cried because he's sad that he disappointed you by breaking it. You're sad that you can't replace it. You make the choice to comfort your child and reassure him it's okay. The vase is not as important as the peace and joy in your mind, soul, and home. That's the power of grace! Mistakes, failures, and poor choices are a part of life. What you do with is up to you. How you extend grace is your choice. The only constant, unwavering, faithful example is the grace of God.

Grace is used often in the church as a godly characteristic and from a biblical perspective concerning the attributes of God. His grace is sufficient; His grace is overflowing. It also used in most Christian homes at the kitchen table or during fellowships before eating. We say Grace, a short prayer and blessing over the food and the preparer and of course to our Father for providing.

The dictionary also defines it several ways. It is defined as simple elegance or refinement of movement, courteous goodwill, an attractively polite manner of behaving, (in Christian belief) the free and unmerited favor of God, as manifested in the salvation of sinners and the bestowal of blessings, or a period officially allowed for payment of a sum due or for compliance with a law or condition, especially an extended period granted as a special favor. As we can see, grace can be used in many different incidents, circumstances, for several purposes.

The number five is a biblical symbolism for God's grace. The Bible details stories of how grace was extended for a purpose. God used grace and unmerited favor to save sinners by giving us His one and only son (John 3:16). Jesus died for us while we were yet sinners. This is His grace in action. There are a host of examples from a biblical perspective of God's grace found in Mark, Matthew, Luke and John. Literally, the Bible's written word is grace embodied.

There is a story in the Bible about a woman caught in adultery. Jesus was speaking, and the Pharisees brought a woman who had been caught in the act of adultery. They put her in front of the crowd. The law of Moses said to stone her, but they wanted to know what Jesus would say. It is amazing how they ignored the understanding of the law to get wisdom and knowledge from the One who came to fulfill the law. They kept demanding an answer, and Jesus finally told them who has never sinned throw the first stone. The accusers left one by one until only Jesus and the woman were left in the middle of the crowd. He asked her, "Where are the accusers, didn't even one condemn you?" The woman said, "No, Lord." Jesus told the woman, "Neither do I. Go and sin no more." (John 8:9-11, NLT)

This is an example of Jesus's love, grace and mercy. As women, there are many things we have done that we are ashamed of and that others are so quick to throw us in front of everyone to be ridiculed. Women are shamed for not being a good enough mama, for being the too perfect mama, for being a stay-at-home mama, for having children out of wedlock, for being the mama always at work and not spending enough time with kids, for not having kids, for having too many kids, for being a single mama, for not being married, for putting their career first, and the list can go on. Who are these accusers? Where are they? Can they really condemn you? There is no condemnation in Jesus. Walk in grace and humility, knowing that other people's accusations or opinions are null and void. It does not matter.

Grace is an act of forgiveness. Jesus is forgiving, so we are made in his image and likeness. We are forgiven. At least we should be obedient to forgive. He has forgiven us and shows His grace and mercy each day. The Bible tells us that His mercies are new every day. Every day is a new beginning—a new and fresh start to right our wrongs, complete unfinished tasks, or simply start a new positive habit. God's grace allows us those opportunities. Remember what Jesus told the woman: "Go and sin no more."

When we eat and fellowship with family, friends, and associates, we are given God's grace of provision. God said, "Behold, I have given you every plant yielding seed that is on the face of all the earth, and every tree with seed in its fruit. You shall have them for food." (Genesis 1:29, ESV) Not only is provision given, this is an opportunity to pray and speak blessings over people. As Christians, we understand and believe that it is a great privilege to nourish our bodies. More importantly, we are given a command that we are not to eat bread alone but to be filled by the words of God. So, let's say grace and be blessed physically and spiritually.

Daily Bread

Here are some scriptures that exemplify the connection between grace and provision:

But he answered, "It is written, "'Man shall not live by bread alone, but by every word that comes from the mouth of God.'" (Matthew 4:4)

And Jesus answered him, "It is written, 'Man shall not live by bread alone.'" (Luke 4:4)

Then he ordered the crowds to sit down on the grass, and taking the five loaves and the two fish, he looked up to heaven and said a blessing. Then he broke the loaves and gave them to the disciples, and the disciples gave them to the crowds. And they all ate and were satisfied. And they took up twelve baskets full of the broken pieces left over. And those who ate were about five thousand men, besides women and children. (Matthew 14:19-21)

And you shall eat and be full, and you shall bless the Lord your God for the good land he has given you. (Deuteronomy 8:10)

And when he had said these things, he took bread, and giving thanks to God in the presence of all, he broke it and began to eat. (Acts 27:35)

So, whether you eat or drink, or whatever you do, do all to the glory of God. (1 Corinthians 10:31)

Now as they were eating, Jesus took bread, and after blessing it broke it and gave it to the disciples, and said, "Take, eat; this is my body." (Matthew 26:26)

Continue steadfastly in prayer, being watchful in it with thanksgiving. (Colossians 4:2)

Give us this day our daily bread. (Matthew 6:11)

Which scripture resonates with you? I suggest you find one to mediate on daily. Let the words of God saturate your spirit, so you can pour out to help your family and others in need. Remember the law of reciprocity. Sow good seeds, so you can reap a harvest of good fruit.

Use the space below to write your thoughts.

Heavenly Father,

We thank You for Your unmerited favor and grace. We thank You for the grace of a new day to start with a new beginning. You are good, and Your mercy endures forever. You have given us another chance to right our wrongs. You have forgiven us by Your grace. Thank You for the provisions to sustain and maintain my life. Thank You for forgiveness. Help me to forgive those who trespass against me or those who intentionally or unintentionally hurt me. In Jesus' name, heal my heart and declutter my mind by Your Spirit. Your grace is sufficient for me to carry on each and every task today. Give us this day our daily bread. Help me to fulfill the purpose You have given me. You know the plans You have for me—plans to prosper me and do good, not harm. I'm trusting in Your word and Your promises. Your word will not return unto You void. I am forgiven by Your grace. Help me to walk in humility and live my life gracefully. I believe I was created for good works. I am ready to receive Your grace this day. I declare and decree I am favored and blessed. I shall prosper, and grace is upon me.

In Jesus' name, Amen.

Why Not You?

Let me introduce you to Jade. Jade is a 42-year-old mama of three kids, all elementary school aged, and wife of a husband who is in a corporate working industry. They are a Christian family and go to church frequently. She volunteers at her kids' school and church. Her husband works full time and sometimes overtime. She works fulltime and is home on the weekends with her family. She occasionally does not have time for herself and seldom hangs out with her friends, and when she does get leisure time, she like coffee dates, and art. She yearns for the divinely connected friendship to meet her emotional needs. Jade enjoys Christian music but still listens to upbeat secular music and loves to dance when no one is looking. Her favorite Christian artists are Tasha Cobbs Leonard, Jekalyn Carr, and William Murphy. Her favorite secular artists are Mary J Blige, Cardi B., India Arie, and some old school classics. She watches Food Network TV, OWN, BET, and HGTV. Her favorite pastime is karaoke, reading, and gardening. Her kids play soccer and participate in football and gymnastics. She likes to cook at home but feels exhausted from work or does not have time to prepare food at a decent hour for her family and sometimes runs out of ideas. At times she feels overwhelm and unorganized and wastes food. Jade doesn't remember her grocery list and sometimes forget to pick up an item. She would rather have things simplified and her life organized for those days she is too busy. Jade is a fictional character for storytelling. Either she is you, or you know someone like Jade. How does Jade serve her family and still manage her wellbeing? Grace.

As women, we have been subjected to a vast array of life circumstances that leave us asking the same question, "Why me?" Have you ever considered asking the question, "Why not me?" I know it's not easy being a caregiver, working outside the home, working from home, volunteering and all the other obligations we busy ourselves with. Have you considered the grace that God gives us freely to live and work? He created us; he knows the very number of our hairs. Why wouldn't he give us the wherewithal to do what he created us to do? The issue we encounter is when we try to juggle it all without Him, without partaking in the grace given to us. I believe Jade is right where she needs to be. She has made God an active part of her life and family. Although she is not fully where she wants to be, Jade is on the path to her destiny. Just like Jade, choose to embrace the journey, and go through the process. We may be at a season in life where we need to be planting or a season where we need to be waiting. The harvest will arrive in due season. In between the time of waiting and harvesting, Jade can effectively use what she has, or outsource. Later, we will discuss what's in your hands.

I'm not just a Christian woman. I am an author, chef, entrepreneur, military veteran, but most importantly, I am a wife and mama. I have a lot going on. I'm sure you do too. I'm multidimensional, just like most of you. I refer to myself as a diamond because a diamond is multifaceted. A diamond is just as beautiful even when its flawed; it still has some shine. A diamond is said to be a woman's best friend. It's not like Jesus to covet, but we sometimes covet a diamond. In all its uniqueness and flaws, it is coveted. Don't doubt your worth and uniqueness, flaws and all.

Jesus encountered the Samaritan woman. She showed up to the well as part of her normal routine. Jesus was tired from his journey and sat by the well. Isn't it something how when we least expect Him to show up, He's there. The Samaritan woman at the well didn't know what she really needed and what she really was looking for in life, yet Jesus knew what she needed better than the woman knew herself. Sometimes we go looking for things that we think we need by searching for love in all the wrong places, seeking attention in purchasing all the wrong things, and doing unnecessary tasks. This, my dear, is a lesson in identity. When we know who we are and understand the power of God's grace, we begin to stand firm in who we were created to be. Maybe we know what is needed, but we don't know why it's needed. Let's call the Samaritan woman Chanya (pronounced Kan-ya) for storytelling purposes. Chanya is Hebrew for Grace of Jehovah. Chanya is asked by Jesus to give Him a drink of water. She didn't understand why a Jewish man would ask her, a Samaritan woman, for a drink. Chanya is questioning, "Of course, He's thirsty but why me?" Jesus answered her saying, "If you knew, the generosity of God and who I am, you would be asking me for a drink, and I would give you fresh living water." Chanya was looking for love in all the wrong places. She was thirsty. Chanya realized she wanted and needed this water. She didn't want to ever not have access to the living water in that well again. The Bible goes on to tell us, in John 4, that the people God is looking for are those who can be honest with themselves before Him in worship. Be your true self in adoration of Him. Chanya was so confused she left her water pot to go tell the people in the village about the man she met who knew her inside and out.

As women, we do a lot to support our family and sustain our well-being. When God purposed us to be helpers, he had our needs in mind and made us fearfully and wonderfully. He knows our capacity because we were uniquely formed in our mothers' wombs. To get a better understanding, let's go back to the beginning when the Lord God took the rib from the man, made woman, and brought her to the man. (Genesis 2:22) I did some research on the human body ribs. The ribs are our protection for vital organs such as the heart and lungs. They also help us to breathe. Take a moment and think about that. God took the most protective bone in man's body to form woman. For a woman to be a helper, she had to be created from something that helps protect the vital organs. We are not made only to help man; we are made to help each other. It's how we survive and thrive. God is intentional. Because He is intentional, we should be intentional.

Women are created purposefully to help. In everything that I do and who I am, I intentionally look for ways to be a helper for family, church, community, and the people who are specifically for me to serve. In my debut book, I write about my journey to finding my purpose through my passions. Once I discovered what specific needs I am called to serve and the gifts I have been entrusted to share, my life became structured to achieve goals that express my calling. As an entrepreneur, I share my gifts to help other families like Jade. If what you are doing is not aligned to your purpose, make goals that are and set out to achieve them. You are given the grace by God to do what is set before you. If you're in a tough situation, ask for wisdom and discernment to get yourself to the blessed place God designed especially for you.

Daily Bread

Here are some scriptures that exemplify the connection between grace and helper:

Then the Lord God said, "It is not good that the man should be alone; I will make him a helper fit for him." (Genesis 2:18)

But he said to me, "My grace is sufficient for you, for my power is made perfect in weakness." Therefore, I will boast all the more gladly of my weaknesses, so that the power of Christ may rest upon me. (2 Corinthians 12:9)

Likewise, wives, be subject to your own husbands, so that even if some do not obey the word, they may be won without a word by the conduct of their wives, (1 Peter 3:1)

An excellent wife who can find? She is far more precious than jewels. The heart of her husband trusts in her, and he will have no lack of gain. She does him good, and not harm, all the days of her life. (Proverbs 31:10-12)

Let us then with confidence draw near to the throne of grace, that we may receive mercy and find grace to help in time of need. (Hebrews 4:16)

Which scripture resonates with you? I suggest you find one to mediate on daily. Let the words of God saturate your spirit, so you can pour out to help your family and others in need. Remember the law of reciprocity. Sow good seeds, so you can reap a harvest of good fruit.

Use the space below to write your thoughts.

Heavenly Father,

I praise You for who You are. You are my Great Jehovah Jireh, always providing for me and my family. Thank You for meeting our every need according to Your word that says You shall supply all my needs. When I feel hopeless and helpless, fill me up with Your Spirit to strengthen me and encourage me in difficult times. Your grace is enough for me. As I carry on each task today, I invite the Holy Spirit to guide me, comfort me, and lead me in the direction I should go. Order my steps; direct my paths; give me wisdom to do each task with grace and humility. You are the Alpha and the Omega; you know the ending before the beginning, so let Your will be done this day. Give me this day, my daily bread. Continually protect my family and bless us and keep us in perfect peace—peace that surpasses all understanding. Thank You, Jesus, for interceding on my behalf as I intercede for those around me. Help us to build one another up and work on one accord as working unto You. In Jesus' name, I pray and believe all things work together for our good. Amen.

You're worth is not found in what you do, Your worth is in who you are.

What's in Your Hands

Let's look into the life of the widow. The Bible doesn't give her a name. We will call her Anna. Anna's husband was a God-fearing man. He died owing debts, and she became a widow with two sons. She loved her sons dearly and didn't want them taken into slavery. Can you imagine not knowing what to do to keep your sons while paying off debts with little to your name. You're having to do all of this without your husband, your life partner, the one you were created for as a help meet? I can imagine that situation—not literally in the sense of your sons taken into slavery but just to keep them fed, a roof over their heads, and a few resources. For the unthinkable to happen and be left on your own to figure things out is scary to imagine. What could you do? First pray, and ask for wisdom, then allow God's grace to sustain you. Anna received wisdom from a man of God name Elisha. She received instructions to use what she had. All she had was a small jar of olive oil, as written in 2 Kings 4. Pay attention to God's grace as you read the story. Anna went around asking neighbors for empty jars. She received the jars she needed and immediately followed Elisha's instructions. She went inside, shut the door behind her, and her sons filled each jar and set it aside.

The olive oil stopped when there were no more jars. She told Elisha, and he said go and sell them to pay your debts.

This story is a reminder that you don't have to worry about what you don't have. Use what you do have, and outsource what you don't have. Anna borrowed jars that she didn't have to return. This is grace and favor working together. Anna and her husband served in their community, so when she borrowed the jars, she received the grace to use them as she desired. This is an example of reciprocity and sowing good seeds. The neighbors knew publicly what she was dealing with, but God was working privately behind the scenes to bless her and her sons. God never asks us for what we don't have. He uses what we do have and equips us for what he purposes. Anna only had a little oil, not enough. Anna was probably thinking, I just lost my husband, I'm on the verge of losing my sons, and you want me to borrow jars and fill with a small amount of olive oil. That's all I have. I can hear in the spirit God telling her like He has told me, "Surrender. Surrender what you do have. I have given you the ability to get wealth." "Will you trust in Me?" says God. "Will you heed the instructions of My prophet?" says God. Empty your hands of what you do have so God can meet your needs.

Anna acted on boldness. She allowed her faith to be activated. Anna didn't know she would receive any jars. Anna neighbors knew her circumstances. Oh, the guilt and shame she must have felt. I was recently in Anna's predicament. I obeyed the prompting of the Holy Spirit to testify about my circumstances, not knowing how God would bring me out. I trusted that He would. I released the circumstance out of my hands, and I surrendered to Him because I had sown seeds. Anna probably thought, "What if this doesn't work?" "What if God won't come through?" Anna is not the only woman who have these thoughts. Let's say grace and cast out any thought that exalts above the knowledge and wisdom of God right now!

What we're holding in our hands is not meant to stay. Our hands are for fluidity and flexibility. Our fingers are attached to our palms individually and separately. Our knuckles are made to bend open and close.

We can grasp and throw away freely. Therefore, we should be intentional about what we pick up and what we hold on to.

Jade and Anna both have insecurities and areas of confidence. They each have different gifts, capabilities, and a different amount of grace given. Jade is a fictional person and Anna, the widow, is a biblical person. We can learn from them both. Jade is a wife and mama, making the best of her abilities and resources through grace. Anna is a widowed mama who made use of her abilities and resources through grace. There are some things Jade can surrender, and she soon will find out as her circumstances lead her. Anna found out through circumstances when she thought that what she had wasn't enough, she surrendered it and was able to be sustained thereafter. I'm sure Jade can surrender it all to God! We can surrender it all to Him too. His word says to cast our cares upon Him for HE CARES FOR US. When there is no one to talk to or no one to listen to us who truly understands, He is there always. God will never leave us, nor forsake us.

Jade is struggling with fear; she does not know yet that she is fearfully and wonderfully made. She read it in scripture. She heard it from her pastor at church and even prayed it in her prayers. For her to know it is a big difference. Sometimes you just don't know what you don't know. She's going to learn really soon.

After reading this chapter, pause and look at your hands. Open your spiritual eyes to see yourself the way God sees you. As stated earlier, you were created fearfully, wonderfully and uniquely. Your fingerprints are not alike any other person on earth. That is amazing! He knows what you can handle. He wants you to give anything you cannot handle to Him. His grace is sufficient! You may think that you don't have enough to do what you must, to fulfill your calling, or take care of your family, but that's far from true. God wants you to release it all. He wants to take the daily, miniscule details of your life and multiply the blessings. How could Jade possibly forget an item from the grocery shopping list that seems too much to schedule.? It happens to the most organized, composed, and smartest woman you know. Do you know any? The same grace you give others is the same grace you give yourself, if not much more. We all have our hands full, but it doesn't have to be that way.

Daily Bread

Here are some scriptures that exemplify the connection between grace and favor:

For by grace you have been saved through faith. And this is not your own doing; it is the gift of God, (Ephesians 2:8)

Therefore, preparing your minds for action, and being sober-minded, set your hope fully on the grace that will be brought to you at the revelation of Jesus Christ. (1 Peter 1:13)

And without faith it is impossible to please him, for whoever would draw near to God must believe that he exists and that he rewards those who seek him. (Hebrews 11:6)

For we are his workmanship, created in Christ Jesus for good works, which God prepared beforehand, that we should walk in them. (Ephesians 2:10)

And God is able to make all grace abound to you, so that having all sufficiency in all things at all times, you may abound in every good work. (2 Corinthians 9:8)

Having gifts that differ according to the grace given to us, let us use them: if prophecy, in proportion to our faith; (Romans 12:6)

Which scripture resonates with you? I suggest you find one to mediate on daily. Let the words of God saturate your spirit, so you can pour out to help your family and others in need. Remember the law of reciprocity. Sow good seeds, so you can reap a harvest of good fruit.

Use the space below to write your thoughts.

Heavenly Father,

You are a gracious God. You work wonders. I stand in awe of Your mighty power. I come before You with my heart open and my hands empty to receive. I surrender it all to You this day. Give me this day, our daily bread. I have gifts according to the grace You have given me. Let me do works in proportion to my faith. Faith without works is dead, so I declare and decree that I am bold; I am resourceful; I am productive, and I succeed in You. I can do all things through Christ who gives me strength. I give you my daily task list. I give you my itinerary. I give you my schedule and appointments. Have your way with them, Abba Father. Holy Spirit, I ask for wisdom, to know the direction I need to take and wisdom to know the things that are not producing fruit in this season. As I abide in you, and Your word abides in me, I shall produce much fruit. God, You are able to make all grace abound to me. Your grace is sufficient. If there is anything not like Your will for my life and my family, remove it now. Shower me with Your grace and favor to continue the good works You have called me to do. Give me the strength to carry on daily tasks. Your strength is made perfect in my weakness. There is power in Your word. Your word is a lamp unto my feet and a light on my pathway. Keep me and guide me. Thank You for Your word. Thank You for Your peace. Thank You for always being with me.

Let Thy will be done. Let Thy kingdom come In Jesus' name, Amen.

Home is Where the Heart Is

The day has been exhausting for Jade. She has experienced much better days. She'd rather go home, kick off her shoes, take off her bra, and recline with a glass of wine or cup of tea, whichever is at home right now. The only problem is Jade must make sure her family has food to eat, and the kids do their homework. Jade practices self-care, so tonight she has a bubble bath with her monthly book reading scheduled. This takes place while she is locked in her bathroom for 30 minutes. She is looking forward to it. Her husband is working late, so he can't help the kids with homework. She forgot to get mozzarella cheese when she made groceries. She needs it to cook "Not Your Mama's Meatloaf," a recipe from *Cooking on Purpose* cookbook. To get to her self-care routine, she must check off everything else on her task list. Jade is cool, calm and collected because Jade has a plan. She outsources what she doesn't have time for and prioritizes everything else. Last week Jade made a schedule and task list. She prays over her task list daily. By doing so Jade can have a comfortable, loving and peaceful environment in her home. Her older son has after school practice, so she prioritizes what needs to be done before she picks him up or after she picks him. She is grateful that her kids are self-sufficient when they care to be. It never ceases to amaze her how they yell "mama" for something so trivial as getting a cup of water. It shouldn't surprise her much when she gave them the house rule, "Don't get anything without asking for it first." Maybe she needs to work a little more on improving that rule.

Your home should be a place of peace, joy, love, and comfort. Your husband should feel joy and anticipate his arrival home. I imagine Jade's husband is just as exhausting as she is after working late. Her kids probably feel the need to get comfortable after sitting in their school desks all day. To keep calm amidst the chaos, Jade relies on God's grace to help her serve her family. God's grace is provided where He abides. He abides in us if we abide in Him, so Jade prays daily and sets an atmosphere for worship in her home. It's not always easy or smooth sailing, but it makes a difference if God is in your home. Let us rewind back to the start of Jade and her family's day.

It's 5:45 a.m. Jade hears the sound of her phone alarm ringing to the tunes of Kurt Carr's "Oh, mighty God, this great congregation of Your people awaits Your Presence. We know that when You come You will bring everything we need, so manifest Your Glory in this place. Touch us, oh God. Bless this house, bless this house, keep us strong." Jade turns off the alarm before the song can finish. She lies down a minute and opens her Bible app, so she can read her daily bread and hear from God. She proceeds out of bed while her kids and husband are still sleeping. After using the bathroom, Jade goes and turns her favorite praise and worship music, William Murphy radio on Pandora. Usually Jade has time for some light cleaning. This morning she forgot her kids' school clothes in the dryer last night, so she immediately takes them out and get them ready for her kids as she wakes them up. Jade and her kids almost always make it just in time to catch the bus. The kids run out as her husband is just waking to let their dog out of the house. Jade now goes into her prayer closet before completing the rest of her day. This routine keeps Jade graceful and her mind renewed. She has so much on her plate. The only wise choice is to eat one thing at a time and savor each bite. Her prayer closet has become her favorite space in the home and is a part of her self-care she didn't make up or even consider it to be. Lately, it's the only consistent thing she does for her emotional wellbeing.

When something doesn't get done, like the laundry the night before, Jade has learned to let it go and start over the next day. His mercies are new every day! Jade knows that prayer will manifest itself as grace in her good works. On some occasions Jade has to pray and fast for wisdom and insight as to how to eat off the plate she has been served. Jade has so many plates. Jade has a plate served with work. She has a plate served with homemaking, a plate served with children's extracurricular activities, and her own hobbies and wellbeing. She also has plate served with church ministry duties. Jade also has a plate served with marital priorities and responsibilities.

Her day doesn't always go as planned. Sometimes the waiter (God) will come, take the plate away, clear the table, and give a new dessert to try. Jade feels she has enough and will get full, but God says, "My grace is sufficient for you." Sometimes wisdom looks like help for you and your home. Sometimes wisdom sounds like thinking, "I can't eat that right now; I will save it for later." If you're at a place Jade has been, remind yourself that it's okay to seek help, and it's also okay to not do anything. If all else fails, Jade has learned tomorrow will be a new day, and she can start over. Her mantra has become, "There are no failures, only lessons." Wherever Jade is called, grace will help her get through.

Your home is a sanctuary for every member of your family. It should not be a place that causes chaos and confusion. As women, and mostly mamas, we all heard the saying, If mama ain't happy, nobody is happy." The statement has truth. You as the keeper of your home must find the sanity and calm you need so that it flows throughout the home. Become naked and unashamed. Go back to Chapter 3 and read it with your spiritual eyes.

Anna became naked and unashamed to get the wisdom and help she needed for her family. Do not be deceived by this world. No one is perfect. We are all flawed, yet wonderfully made. When Eve was in the Garden of Eden with Adam, they were surrounded with beauty and peace. All their needs were met. We should make our homes like the Garden of Eden.

Learn from the mistake Eve made. She was disobedient, which resulted in confusion. We as women, are the weaker vessels when it comes to attacks from the enemy. It's hard not to be tempted, but be careful to take the way of escape. It's presented before us if we open our eyes spiritually. We can easily become blindsided and play the blame game. We can blame it on our spouses all we want to, but God will hold us accountable to the one whom He gave instructions. Another lesson in that is to let the man lead. Submit! We can dismiss chaos and confusion when we know our role and play our role. Ouch, that may have hurt a little, but sometimes the truth hurts when it's right. Don't try to be everything to everybody or do anything without God's grace. Remember Anna. She was wise in using God's grace. She solicited the help of her sons. The family as a whole contributed to make a way.

When I was growing up in my mama's home, we had chores. If you are like Jade, and you want to let grace abide, consider how you can prioritize and delegate. Now would be a good time to pray about direction for chores and tasks in your home. Set aside a schedule to get everyone involved in helping.

Daily Bread

Here are some scriptures that exemplify the connection between grace and homemaking:

> *But he said to me, "My grace is sufficient for you, for my power is made perfect in weakness." Therefore, I will boast all the more gladly of my weaknesses, so that the power of Christ may rest upon me.* (2 Corinthians 12:9)

> *You then, my child, be strengthened by the grace that is in Christ Jesus.* (2 Timothy 2:1)

> *But he gives more grace. Therefore, it says, "God opposes the proud, but gives grace to the humble."* (James 4:6)

> *But as for you, teach what accords with sound doctrine. Older men are to be sober-minded, dignified, self-controlled, sound in faith, in love, and in steadfastness. Older women likewise are to be reverent in behavior, not slanderers or slaves to much wine. They are to teach what is good, and so train the young women to love their husbands and children, to be self-controlled, pure, working at home, kind, and submissive to their own husbands, that the word of God may not be reviled.* (Titus 2:1-5)

> *Now may our Lord Jesus Christ himself, and God our Father, who loved us and gave us eternal comfort and good hope through grace, encourage your hearts and strengthen you in every good deed and word.* (2 Thessalonians 2:16-17)

> *For by grace you have been saved through faith. And this is not your own doing; it is the gift of God, not a result of works, so that no one may boast. For we are his workmanship, created in Christ Jesus for good works, which God prepared beforehand, that we should walk in them.* (Ephesians 2:8-10)

> *And I am sure of this, that he who began a good work in you will bring it to completion at the day of Jesus Christ.* (Philippians 1:6)

And from his fullness we have all received, grace upon grace. (John 1:16)

She is clothed with strength and dignity; she can laugh at the days to come. She speaks with wisdom, and faithful instruction is on her tongue. She watches over the affairs of her household and does not eat the bread of idleness. Her children arise and calls her blessed; her husband also, and he praises her. Many women do noble things, but you surpass them all. (Proverbs 31:25-29, NIV)

Which scripture resonates with you? I suggest you find one to mediate on daily. Let the words of God saturate your spirit, so you can pour out to help your family and others in need. Remember the law of reciprocity. Sow good seeds so you can reap a harvest of good fruit.

Use the space below to write your thoughts.

Heavenly Father,

You are Jehovah Jireh, my provider. Thank You for being a provider of all that I want and need. Thank You being Creator of all things. You created the heavens, earth, and man. You saw that it was very good. You created me for helping, You called me to be a homemaker. You have given me the grace to serve. Create in a me a clean heart renew in me a right spirit so that I may always have a servant's mindset in my home. I am clothed with strength and dignity; I can laugh at the days to come because You cover me in grace. Help me through Your Holy Spirit to watch over the affairs of my household. My children call me blessed; my husband praises me. And I am sure of this, that he who began a good work in me will bring it to completion at the day of Jesus Christ. The battle is already won. I have the victory in my struggles. I have the victory in my home. I have the victory in my work. I have the victory in my marriage. I will not be defeated by the enemy's tactics. Temptation comes, but Jesus came that we have life more abundantly and that we live by every word of God. The word says I am blessed and more than a conqueror. I have never seen the righteous forsaken or his seed begging bread. Father, thank You for being a provider. Thank You for being the source of everything my family needs. Keep my husband covered that he may lead and guide our family into righteousness. What You have joined together, let no man put asunder. My husband is the head and not the tail. Help me to submit to his authority under you God. A threefold cord is not easily broken. You honor marriages. Give us what we need to make our home complete in You.

Let Thy will be done in Jesus' mighty name, Amen.

A Wise Woman Builds

You know a little about me and who I am based on my social media profile and by googling "Chef Diana Riley." Maybe you heard of me as an author and chef from someone else right now, you are probably thinking about the fact that I have a husband and five kids. Either you're thinking or have already said one or two things about me: 1) "You must have your hands full," or 2) "You have help in the home and in life; you got it made." Let me keep it real, I don't have it all together, as a matter of fact, nobody does. I'm a pretty mess but thank God for His grace.

You're reading this, and you may have had somebody think that of you. I know I'm not the only who thinks that people say, "You're doing too much. I don't know how you can do it." Or maybe you heard, "You have help. Get the kids to do chores. Your husband is a good provider, so you should not need anything else." In some cases, this is so not true! Make no assumptions; gratefulness is still much alive in my life. I am grateful for every gift and blessing, and I'm assured you are grateful too. I have had people tell me that I have a lot going on and calling me busy. I'm not busy, I'm productive. What they see and have not realized yet, is God's grace working through me in my life. I have lots of downtime with my family! God created us help meets, but we all still need help. Our hands are not full when we abide in God's grace. It doesn't matter what anyone else thinks or says. It matters what God says and does. He is able to do exceedingly abundantly above anything we ask or think.

Anna needed help, and she knew she needed help. Anna also knows she has what is required to help her and her family. After her husband passes away, she is left with debt and two kids to take care of. How could she possibly do it alone? She cried to Elisha for help. That was a cry heard by God who orchestrated the help she needed. Being a Christian does not exempt you from the trials of life. When the trials come, it is how you handle them that determines the outcome. Be of good cheer! You can rely on self, or you can rely on God. It's your choice. God sends us people. God gives us resources. Character is more valuable; relationships are meaningful, and life is more important. Don't give in to the pressure and don't you dare give up on yourself. You have everything you need.

Anna took the little she had, that was treasured and desired in her time, to produce the harvest she needed in her life at the time and for the future. Anna wasn't too proud to beg. She humbled herself to continue to be the help meet for her family. We are women of God. We are His daughters, and He takes care of our needs. Women of God uses godly principles and behaviors to build a life that God desires us to have.

Anna knew deep down in her soul that her situation couldn't be the end of her life. Anna knew that God wouldn't give up on her, so she couldn't give up on her life. Anna used her resources to sustain, overcome, and build her future by grace. Realizing that all Anna had was a small jar of olive oil was all she needed proves God will take what you have and multiply it. Remember the five fish and two loaves of bread that fed 5000. You, woman of God are the knowledge and resource. You are the help and gift. God has equipped you to influence, impact, teach, and create.

Anna was used to influence and teach in the time of need. Anna influenced her neighbors to help her in a time of trouble. Anna became a resource of inspiration. She gave her neighbors an example of God stepping in on time and delivering her and her family out of poverty. If God did it for Anna certainly, He can do it for us. Anna was used to teach her sons. She instructed her sons to help her ask for jars and help her fill them. She was teaching them a work ethic. She was teaching them responsibility, and she was teaching them liberation. Anna taught her sons the importance of using what you have to work for what you want. Her sons knew they only had one small jar of olive oil that wasn't enough for them. They learned if they work to get more, they can have what they want and need. Anna was obedient to the instructions given to her when she asked. More than likely, her sons were not responsible for much at home. In the same way Jade is teaching her kids responsibility. Maybe Jade's kids have to help their father with yardwork or take out the trash. Of course, they must go to school and do homework. Mamas like you and I know that's not much responsibility compared to providing your children's basic life necessities such as, food, shelter, health. That day, Anna's sons learned how to be responsible for much more than themselves. They had a responsibility to keep the family together. Liberation is something that we gain an understanding in our minds first. We all are free, but who the Son sets free is free indeed. Anna and her sons were set free from lack and poverty that day. They came to know that God answers prayer. The one act of obedience gave her entire family and community deliverance. Anna's sons discovered that working together as a team and relying on faith will set them free from their circumstances. God used Anna as an example of public shame being turned into private prayers being answered openly. He gave her beauty for ashes. Not everyone is privy of the process. That's why Anna was instructed to close the doors behind her. God was working on the inside and behind the scenes. Nobody had to know how He did it. Shucks, Anna probably don't even know how he did it. After all, she only had one jar of oil. Precious treasure and oil are in a wise man's dwelling, but a foolish man devours it. (Proverbs 21:10, ESV)

Use Anna as an example to be the kind of woman that stands her ground and does not give up in tough situations. Anna took what she had to build what she needed. She used her sons to help her and relied on her neighbors to help her in a time of trouble. Anna didn't give up when she lost her husband and was on the verge of losing everything she owned, including her sons. Anna thought she had nothing that could get her out of her circumstances. Anna is a wise woman who builds.

You and I may not be experiencing the same circumstances as Anna, but we can learn from Anna. What do we have right now to build the life we want; the abundant life God calls us to live? Like me, you are the head not the tail, above and not beneath. Are you using your influence to build your children's courage and confidence? It starts at home. Are you using your godly wisdom to support your spouse? Can you be trusted to keep the family legacy? Are you impacting your community with your gifts and talents? Are you using the resources available to you to set your family free from lack, poverty, illness, and setbacks? You and I were created for good works. Our first ministry is our family and home. We ought to worship God in spirit and in truth in everything that we do. Let's continue to help build our family's legacy and God's kingdom with grace.

Daily Bread

Here are some scriptures that exemplify the connection between grace and work:

A wife of noble character who can find? She is worth far more than rubies. Her husband has full confidence in her and lacks nothing of value. (Proverbs 31:10-11, NIV)

She selects wool and flax and works with eager hands. (Proverbs 31:13)

But grow in the grace and knowledge of our Lord and Savior Jesus Christ. To him be the glory both now and to the day of eternity. Amen. (2 Peter 3:18, ESV)

I appeal to you therefore, brothers, by the mercies of God, to present your bodies as a living sacrifice, holy and acceptable to God, which is your spiritual worship. Do not be conformed to this world, but be transformed by the renewal of your mind, that by testing you may discern what is the will of God, what is good and acceptable and perfect. (Romans 12:1-2)

Let us then with confidence draw near to the throne of grace, that we may receive mercy and find grace to help in time of need. (Hebrews 4:16)

And now I commend you to God and to the word of His grace, which is able to build you up and to give you the inheritance among all those who are sanctified. (Acts 20:32)

And after you have suffered a little while, the God of all grace, who has called you to his eternal glory in Christ, will himself restore, confirm, strengthen, and establish you. (1 Peter 5:10)

What shall we say then? Are we to continue in sin that grace may abound? (Romans 6:1)

Working together with him, then, we appeal to you not to receive the grace of God in vain. (2 Corinthians 6:1)

But I do not account my life of any value nor as precious to myself, if only I may finish my course and the ministry that I received from the Lord Jesus, to testify to the gospel of the grace of God. (Acts 20:24)

Which scripture resonates with you? I suggest you find one to mediate on daily. Let the words of God saturate your spirit, so you can pour out to help your family and others in need. Remember the law of reciprocity. Sow good seeds so you can reap a harvest of good fruit.

Use the space below to write your thoughts.

Mind Your Business

Jade has enough going on in her life that she has no time to worry about anything else. When the pressure gets low in one of her tires, she now has to check it before it goes flat because her husband is out of town for work. On top of that, the dog is out of food, and the school called to set up a parent-teacher conference. Meanwhile, her sister is having a crisis and needs her listening ear, and one of her friends is having money and man problems. Jade thinks to herself, "Ain't nobody got time for that!"

Jade is focusing her thoughts on what is good and what is right, but every now and then something comes along to distract her. The mere fact that she knows she can barely eat the food on her plate, much less someone else's, is a strength. Why attempt to take on someone's else issues? She has leftovers from yesterday waiting on her today and probably tomorrow! It is much better for her to stay in her lane.

The Bible states that the enemy comes to kill, steal and destroy. The enemy sometimes comes in the form of distractions. Don't be deceived. Don't be misled. You have the power and the authority to defeat the enemy. It's your choice.

Jade has a big vision, and the only way to accomplish it is to focus on small goals and prioritizing. It is okay to be selfish. At this time in her life, Jade needs to be selfish. She is very selfless in taking care of her kids and supporting her husband. Being selfish does not mean she does not care about her family. Her being selfish does not mean she does not want to help others, being selfish for her means she has learned to take care of herself better and prioritize her needs favorable to her vision. Now is not time to get out of alignment. The time now is to set her face straight like flint and go after her dreams and chase the vision she cast. As a visionary you must impart the vision and have faith to see it accomplished, whether you're working alone or if you're blessed with a team. Never settle for anything less than what God told you to do.

Sometimes you may fall into the trap of helping others, or worst-case scenario comparing yourself to what others are doing or what they have. My dear, that is the easiest way to lose momentum and become discouraged. Mind your business. Your circle may need to be so small that only one person can fit into it. Jade has so much experience being by herself to the point that if an acquaintance invited her to a coffee date, she felt uncomfortable enough to the point of declining. It's imperative that you as a woman discern who you allow in your life as you learn to align your purpose with family. Some people add value while others subtract. God can't multiply your efforts if you are continually taking away from what he has given you to steward. To be a friend, you must first learn how to be the friend. Jade is making personal development a priority, so she can be a whole person ready to fill and be filled.

Your business is not going to take care of itself, literally and figurately. Your business needs a Chief Executive Officer, Manager, Supervisor, Boss, Mamapreneur, whatever you want to call yourself. Your "business" is your ministry. I researched the definition of business, and this is what I discovered. Business is a commercial or sometimes an industrial enterprise which includes transactions, especially of an economic nature. It contains serious activity requiring time and effort and usually the avoidance of distractions, a role, function, an affair or matters of personal concern. What are you doing right now in life that is your business that relates to your ministry?

Jade is a devoted wife and a hardworking mama. She volunteers, and she has a career. Jade has a lot of business to take care of. Her ministry is to help meet the needs of her husband and to support the family while simultaneously fulfilling Jade's purpose. Her business is being the person God created her to be. This is something that sometimes has to be learned through experience. As Maya Angelou said, "When you know better, do better." You can't be all things to everybody and then have little to nothing for yourself. You can't keep pouring from an empty cup. If you want to have meaningful relationships, I believe you must first learn to love self. Jade cannot give what she does not have; likewise, you can't either. Jade will encounter personal challenges in her marriage where a "My Date" is necessary, and self-love will create healing.

My charge to you as a woman fearfully and wonderfully made is to schedule a "My Date" on the calendar. "My Date" is a day set aside just for you, whatever you want or need to do to show yourself love and appreciation. "My Date" is the refilling and renewal you so desperately need to continue your ministry.

Daily Bread

Here are some scriptures that exemplify the connection between grace and self-care:

"Do you not know that you are God's temple and that God's Spirit dwells in you?" (1 Corinthians 3:16)

"God is within her; she will not fall; God will help her at break of day." (Psalm 46:5, NIV)

"And he said to them, "Come away by yourselves to a desolate place and rest a while." For many were coming and going, and they had no leisure even to eat." (Mark 6:31, ESV)

For no one ever hated his own flesh, but nourishes and cherishes it, just as Christ does the church, because we are members of his body. (Ephesians 5:29-30)

She is clothed with strength and dignity; she can laugh at the days to come. She speaks with wisdom, and faithful instruction is on her tongue. She watches over the affairs of her household and does not eat the bread of idleness. (Proverbs 31:25-27, NIV)

"Do not be anxious about anything, but in everything by prayer and supplication with thanksgiving let your requests be made known to God. And the peace of God, which surpasses all understanding, will guard your hearts and your minds in Christ Jesus. Finally, brothers, whatever is true, whatever is honorable, whatever is just, whatever is pure, whatever is lovely, whatever is commendable, if there is any excellence, if there is anything worthy of praise, think about these things." (Philippians 4:6-8, ESV)

Which scripture resonates with you? I suggest you find one to mediate on daily. Let the words of God saturate your spirit, so you can pour out to help your family and others in need. Remember the law of reciprocity. Sow good seeds, so you can reap a harvest of good fruit.

Use the space below to write your thoughts.

*Build the Table,
Set the Table,
Steward the Table*

Plant Your Garden

Jade goes out to run some errands and check off a few items on her task list for the day. While out she feels a nudge to stop at the local Home Depot for some seeds. She purchases lavender, cucumber, green beans, and pumpkin seeds. She goes home and puts a pack of lavender seeds on her desk to remind her of the seeds she has sown. She goes about the rest of her day. As the weeks go by, she could not decide when, where and how she was going to plant the other seeds. She put the task aside. She has learned that when she doesn't know what to do, the best thing is to do nothing. She could not decide whether to pot the seeds or plant them in the ground. Finally, she decides to test the seeds in the ground.

As the days continue passing, Jade forgets about the seeds she had sown. She does not remember the things she has done good or not so good. One day Jade comes home from work, and she notices some unusual leaves like a vine growing near the steps of the front porch. She stops to take notice and get a closer look. Jade had no idea of what she planted or what the plant was. It was as though she had forgotten who she was and didn't recognize herself. It puzzles her so much she googles the image after taking a picture with her iPhone camera. She puts "pumpkin flowers" in the Google search engine because she thought it could be the pumpkin seeds. Jade thinks to herself, "When and why would I put them there?" Who knows, maybe her two younger curious and active kids did. Sure enough, Google confirms they were pumpkin. Jade immediately gets a revelation. All she had to do was plant the seeds. Seeds only produce in the soil. They cannot become what they are designed to become if they stay in the package and are not placed in the right environment. They need dirt, water, sunlight and love. Like Jade, you are like a seed and should embrace the dirt needed to help you grow. Water your soil with the Word. Get enough exposure of His love given through His Son. Every plant has some care instructions; find out exactly what you need and how to nurture yourself to thrive in the environment you belong.

Fascinated by the revelation, Jade has to share the excitement with her husband. As they were acknowledging the plant and discussing the details, she notices the pumpkin flower looks frail. She expresses her concern to her husband. He gives wise advice and tells her that she needs to start taking care of it. The plant needs water now that its growing. Until then, Jade never gave it water. She immediately references the scripture, "I planted; Apollos watered it, but God has been making it grow" as it is written in 1Corinthians 3:6.

Wow! Let's pause and think about that for a moment. Can you imagine the emotion Jade was feeling after the wisdom she received?

From that point on Jade carefully viewed the plant spiritually and aligned its growth with her life and the blessings she had and will receive. Sometimes we need a spiritual overview to put things in perspective. It's not always what it looks like. Walk by faith and not by sight. The pumpkin plant reminded Jade so much of a dream she had a year prior. She dreamed of a pumpkin plant, but when she opened it, sweet potato vines were on the inside. That sounds like a mysterious dream. God was definitely trying to tell her something! God will choose the foolish things of the world to shame the wise. It is not supposed to make sense when God is in it. Did it make sense for Abraham to sacrifice his only son? He didn't want to, but he obeyed. Did it make sense for Ruth to follow Naomi, her mother-in-law, after her husband died? She was free to choose what she wanted to do, and she chose to follow Naomi. Did it make sense for Esther, an adopted orphan, to be queen? She probably was despised because of the label placed on her, but she was favored by God. God chose those despised by the world so they cannot boast about their own doing but only about Him. God gave them each grace in every situation.

Gardening is such a supernatural experience. There is nothing we as humans can do physically to make a seed sprout. What we can do is nurture and support the environment for the seed to sprout. My pastor once said that a seed is only potential until it's planted. That is a powerful revelation. Think about it for a moment. You probably have a pack of seeds in your garage or backyard shed waiting to be planted to become some tasty green beans or a delicious pumpkin pie. It won't become that until you put it in its proper environment conducive for its intended purpose. Then you harvest what you have sown at the right time. We'll discuss that later.

Each and every member of your family has an intended purpose, a calling worth pressing towards. That is where we thrive, where we are fulfilled and are resourceful. The seed will do what it needs to do and what it was created to do when we plant it, water it, and support it. The wonderful revelation I received earlier this year was to water the soil where the seed was sown. From a biblical perspective, we sow seeds in many different areas. We may sow seeds into a needy family during the holidays. We sow seeds in our churches. We sow seeds in other people's ministries or businesses. We sow seeds into our own families. The seed can be in the form of money, time, service, or an item. The seed is a blessing, and we expect a harvest or in laymen terms a return on our investment. How do we know if we're going to receive a harvest or a return? It's simple. Did we sow a "good seed" from our hearts? The Bible calls this being a cheerful giver. Did we sow into "good soil"? Good soil is someone or something capable of producing or benefiting from our seeds. Remember, the only thing we can do to the seed to cause it to sprout is to nurture the environment.

In gardening, sometimes the ground needs to be tilled, and sometimes we have to add organic soil. Most importantly, we must water it.

Our gardens are our families, visions, businesses, and ministries. Our gardens will not come until we sow the seeds. The seeds will not sprout until we plant them. Once planted, we can support them by creating a nurturing environment. Nurturing is cultivating and developing. Whatever seeds we sow, we should be sure to cover them in prayer.

Anna planted a garden by teaching her sons, work ethic and helping to build their character and integrity. Jade is planting a garden through her family. Every day she is taking care of them. Her family will yield a harvest and a return on the investment she is sowing. She expects her children to be a blessing and her husband to be praised. She expects her family to appreciate her and reward her. Remember in the last chapter, I stated Jade can't give what she does not have. Well, Jade is giving what she has in time, support, her gifts and service. In doing so, her family can give back. It's the law of reciprocity. The statement is true; you reap what you sow. What are you sowing?

At this point, Jade is also struggling with her identity, and she is starting to find ways to discover herself again. She has been sowing into her husband and her kids' lives. She always seems to feel like superwoman after rescuing them out of their mess. Now who is going to rescue Jade out of her mess? Although it's a rhetorical question, she really needs and desires to know God's will and His plan to get it right. She desires to do everything right. Perfection has always been her kryptonite. It is slowly diminishing her energy and mood. It's showing up as her harvest.

Daily Bread

Here are some scriptures that exemplify the connection between grace and identity:

Therefore, if anyone is in Christ, he is a new creation. The old has passed away; behold, the new has come. (2 Corinthians 5:17)

Now you are the body of Christ and individually members of it. (1 Corinthians 12:27)

To put off your old self, which belongs to your former manner of life and is corrupt through deceitful desires, and to be renewed in the spirit of your minds, and to put on the new self, created after the likeness of God in true righteousness and holiness. (Ephesians 4:22-24)

Know that the Lord, He is God! It is he who made us, and we are his; we are his people, and the sheep of his pasture. (Psalm 100:3)

In him we have redemption through his blood, the forgiveness of our trespasses, according to the riches of His grace. (Ephesians 1:7)

Which scripture resonates with you? I suggest you find one to mediate on daily. Let the words of God saturate your spirit, so you can pour out to help your family and others in need. Remember the law of reciprocity. Sow good seeds so you can reap a harvest of good fruit.

Use the space below to write your thoughts.

It's Harvest Time

We can't plant a lemon tree and expect apples. It's naturally impossible. It goes against the law of nature. Spiritually, it's impossible; it goes against God's law of reaping and harvesting. We reap what we sow. (Galatians 6:7) Jade has been taking care of everyone, but now she realizes that she needs a return on her investment. How is that going to show up? Well, we all know that there is a season for everything, and sometimes that doesn't show up when we want it to. We have to wait for the right time—in due season. Apples are harvested in fall. Green beans are harvested all summer. Until then, they are not ready to be consumed and enjoyed.

Occasionally, Jade can get her kids to participate in the daily home routines like cleaning up after themselves. Most of the time Jade still helps them. Remember the kids ages; they should be doing this most of the time. Jade often tells them pick up their mess and brush their teeth before bed. She regularly asks, "Did you throw your trash in the garbage?" At this point in her life, Jade needs some relief. Jade consistently tells and reinforces these things with her kids, but she has also been doing it for them. Jade would come into her home and see snack paper on the kitchen table or the play area and pick it up. One day Jade realizes, this is too much, and it is not her responsibility to clean mess and throw trash away she had no part in making in the first place. Her aha moment was the day she started wiping the kitchen table, and something popped in her mind: "Jade, girl you have been doing this too much for too long, stop!" She yelled out to her kids, "Everybody get in here now, and clean this mess you made, RIGHT NOW!" She realized she had told them the rules and what she expects. They know better. Now, it's time to let them do it; don't keep doing it for them. Kids need accountability just like adults. Teach them responsibility, and let them go. Guide them along the way. Most importantly, pray for them, and let God cover them. Mama needed to sit back and enjoy the fruit of her labor.

Jade's marriage is now a challenge. Jade questions God about why her prayers haven't been answered. Jade has been seeking professional therapy. She relies on the comfort, wise counsel, and prayers of her amazing, trustworthy, and patient mentors, friends, and prayer partners. It is a beautiful thing when you have people in your life, who are divinely connected and purposeful that you can reciprocate love, friendship and mentorship. Jade is thankful for those people, and she prays God blesses them daily for pouring out into her. This is part of the harvest Jade is receiving for sowing good seeds into other's life by sharing wise advice and praying for others in difficult times. She is definitely reaping a good harvest in that area of her life in due season.

Jade would probably be in an unfavorable position without the grace of mentors, close friends, and prayer partners. God knows how to give you just what you need when you need it. He strategically placed these people in Jade's life for such a time as this. Her marriage has been flipped upside down for the 13th time in all the years of her marriage. She doesn't know what to do or how to do it. Only because Jade is a praying woman and wants directions from the Holy Spirit, she finds comfort and peace in the people she trusts to help her learn to depend on God. Leaning on God and trusting in Him can be a difficult thing, and Jade has found this to be true when she was faced with yet another tough decision. Jade has many questions: "Do I separate from my husband? I don't want to separate my family, but how do I continue to live in an emotionally unstable position? What will be my kids' reaction? Where do I go, or should he go? Why weren't my prayers answered for deliverance and restoration all the other times in my marriage? If so, why was the restoration if any, short lived?" See, Jade thought God was healing and restoring her marriage after the 8th, 9th, 10th, 11th, 12th time.

It wasn't until now, the 13th time, Jade found refuge in her story to tell somebody, what her marriage was really like. On the outside, it was "perfect." At times, it definitely felt that way. She had lots of joyous and happy occasions in her marriage. She just couldn't seem to understand why her husband didn't respect the sanctity of their marriage enough to not be faithful and commit to fidelity. Shocking! I know you're probably going to go back and read Chapters 2 and 3 just to see how well put together Jade's home life was or look for clues to see this coming. Well, Jade didn't have any clues either, so she naively thought. But the clues were there from early behavior. So, why didn't Jade reap a harvest of unconditional love, care, devotion and fidelity in spite of the fact that was all she gave these many years of marriage. Jade doesn't know either.

Is it her season for harvest? Certainly one would think so. Jade has been consistently faithful—the good wife, cooking, cleaning, supporting the entire household, encouraging her husband and kids, keeping up a peaceful home. What happened, what went wrong? Part of the problem for Jade's husband is the same problem for Jade's kids. Jade has been cleaning up messes she didn't make. Jade now has yet another aha moment, and epiphany. Jade realizes that she can't be the only one working to save her marriage. She was called to be a help meet, not an enabler. Jade has been an enabler. Google defines enabler as "a person or thing that makes something possible, a person who encourages or enables negative or self-destructive behavior in another." Wow! It took the 13th time to know that was the missing link to grow healthy fruit. Sometimes you just have to let people grow on their own. It is not your job to change them. It is your job to nurture them, and let the fruit fall where it may.

Have you ever had the opportunity to plant and grow a fruit tree? For example, a fig tree takes time. Everything takes time. When the fig tree is in its full growth maturity, it produces figs. Notice that some figs are rotten, or over ripe. Some figs are under ripe, or not ready. Most figs are ripe and ready. Sometimes the rotten or overripe fall to the ground. You have the choice to leave it there. You don't have to harvest something that is not ready or not good.

Of course, Jade didn't agree with this behavior. She knew it was wrong and that she didn't have to accept it. She also knows that she took her marriage vows seriously, for better or for worse. She also believes in the Word of God and His precepts. Forgive those who trespass against you. How could she ask for grace and forgiveness if she is not willing to extend that same grace and forgiveness? Jade trusts in God and is leaning not on her understanding until the very end. She is looking for the godly response. She continues to operate in grace and humility to maintain the peace and love in her home, all the while falling apart on the inside because she is not having her emotional needs met. She continues letting her light shine because her joy doesn't come from worldly happenings but from the Spirit. Jade is in a hard place in her life. We are about to uncover the mask that Jade like so many of us are wearing.

This is Jade's winter season yet again. Hardly anything grows in the winter. She has new hopes and ideas that have not come into fruition. She is being tested in order to grow. In the winter, it's the coldest, darkest, most barren time of the year. Everything just seems dead! The seeds are buried in the ground. It's dark, but transformation is happening. God is hiding her process, and the construction site is covered. Jade is working towards a point of a new identity in Christ. He is mending the broken pieces. The first step in the process for Jade is to surrender. When surrendering the project called "You," God, the project manager, has control and responsibility of the finished product.

This is the time for Jade to rest, and let God do the work. Jade has to release the control. For too long Jade has tried to fix and help her family, to little avail, but with much success as well. She counts it all joy because the good times have been prevalent. They don't need fixing by her. She needs to know her identity. Jade knows how to "be still and know that He is God." She understands "To everything there is a season, a time for every purpose under heaven." (Ecclesiastes 3:1) Just because its Summer doesn't mean that Jade can't experience a winter season during the month of July. This is exactly what Jade had been experiencing. What Jade has learned is that just because she planted a seed and expects a harvest, it doesn't necessarily mean she's not going to receive a harvest. The harvest has to be in due season. It has partly to do with the work in caring and cultivation of the seed. We must prune the bad fruit, the bad stems or just pull up the roots. A green plant's beauty can shine better when the dead leaves are pruned away.

Is her waiting in vain? Perhaps. Should she dig up the roots and start over? Possibly. This winter season for the 13th time is the time for Jade to understand why she is here and another opportunity to get it right, so she can reap a harvest of good fruit. She now has to take time to reflect, plan and prepare for what's next. Rest in God's love and intimacy, so He can give directions for the planting of new crops. This is the one thing Jade was lacking the other 12 times. Yes, Jade is a prayer warrior, an intercessor, and has a relationship with Jesus, but Jade was also not releasing all of her burdens and cares to Jesus. She was still operating in grace, but her grace was limited to where she relinquished the control. God gave her grace to endure the pain, but He has so much in store to do exceedingly more than what Jade asks. Jade has been praying daily for her husband, their marriage, and the family as a whole. Her family has been blessed and prosperous. She couldn't imagine how much more she could be blessed if the family unit was separated. Is the pruning process for her marriage separation? That is the one thing Jade has not done during these times of marital infidelity and difficulty. Jade remains sure of herself and confident that her marriage can move on without separation.

As she is gracefully broken, she is sustained. Her children are still being taken care of. Her husband still works and comes home to a clean and peaceful environment. She is still progressing despite the enemy's attacks. Her winter is dark, but there is still hope and light shining. She prays and cries. She does all the things of a good wife, yet she is lonely.

One of the enemy's scheme has been temptation, and she finds herself eating from the forbidden fruit. One of her many questions is, "Why would God allow this?". She wonders what God is trying to tell her. This is the season Jade falls while under construction. His grace is still enough. During these growing pains, she continues to fast, seek wisdom, and learn. Instead of insisting her husband gets help or try, she's quiet and continues to seek therapy for herself. Instead of being the initiator to find solutions to their marriage woes, she continually prays and rests. She is expecting the same grace that she extends to others. Instead of focusing on why this is happening, she understands this is happening for a reason that has a purpose. Jade has left her winter season, the darkest time of her life. She went from discovering infidelity to moving forward to spring and finding a new discovery of herself and a new career.

When Jade enters her spring season, this is the time to plant and follow instructions God has given her. Remember, spring is not predicated on the actual time of spring in the natural. This is a spiritual season indicated by circumstances and environment. The necessary energy and fortitude will be provided to break up the fallow ground. For a long time, 13 times to be exact, Jade was filled with fear and overwhelm. Thank God for His Grace. Jade decides to move from a place of fear and defeat to a place of focus and victory. She is using her God given authority and power to break the bondages. She is carefully discerning which new adventures and relationships to participate in knowing that just like the fig tree some fruit will not be good. Soon she will be in summer possessing a greater anointing and a new level of personal development. This is the time to water what has been planted and prune what should not have been.

Jade can't skip any steps in the process. She can't successfully move forward without completing each step and following the instructions. She must stay tuned to the prompting of the Holy Spirit. Jade has been doing her best to avoid distractions. She wasn't social, in fact she had no social life outside of church. She never went to places that were not ordained for her to be. Now that Jade has done personal work in her life, she can enjoy the harvest and store up for the winter season. The fruit is ripe and ready to be picked. Storing up helps her carry on in times of need. This is now the fall season in Jade's life where there is abundance and a season of encouragement. She can return to her old routines and the newly created routines, and the kids are going back to school. It is a new beginning and an ending to the old. This is the Season of Thanksgiving.

Unlike Jade, sometimes our lives are in sync with the actual physical natural season. It is imperative that we know and understand the season we are in. Jade didn't know what season she was in. For 13 years she was in a never-ending cycle of the same ole same old. Could you imagine planting the same seed every season and not reaping a single fruit from it year after year? How many times are you going to plant a cucumber seed, water it, and wait in expectation of harvest only to find that not one cucumber grew. It's time for a time out! Reflect and journal what you did and didn't do. Maybe you didn't check the PH balance of the soil. Maybe you didn't cover the seeds properly. Maybe you didn't take the environment into consideration. Did it receive enough sunlight? Whatever it is, you must do something differently to expect a different result.

This is the last chapter. Commit to spend time and put forth effort unlearning old habits and letting go of old ways to develop new ways and a new mindset. You are filled with His grace. Know your identity and learn your capacity. Be ready to embark on the new beginning. Plant a garden and nurture it as you nurture yourself and family. It's never too late to start something new and different. Behold old things have passed away, all things are new.

Daily Bread

Here are some scriptures that exemplify the connection between grace and surrender:

I know, Lord, that our lives are not our own. We are not able to plan our own course. (Jeremiah 10:23, NIV)

"Come to me, all you who are weary and burdened, and I will give you rest. (Matthew 11:28)

Going a little farther, he fell with his face to the ground and prayed, *"My Father, if it is possible, may this cup be taken from me. Yet not as I will, but as you will."* (Matthew 26:39)

Trust in the Lord with all your heart and lean not on your own understanding; in all your ways submit to him, and he will make your paths straight. (Proverbs 3:5-6)

I am the true vine, and my Father is the gardener. He cuts off every branch in me that bears no fruit, while every branch that does bear fruit, he prunes so that it will be even more fruitful. 3 You are already clean because of the word I have spoken to you. Remain in me, as I also remain in you. No branch can bear fruit by itself; it must remain in the vine. Neither can you bear fruit unless you remain in me. "I am the vine; you are the branches. If you remain in me and I in you, you will bear much fruit; apart from me you can do nothing. If you do not remain in me, you are like a branch that is thrown away and withers; such branches are picked up, thrown into the fire and burned. If you remain in me and my words remain in you, ask whatever you wish, and it will be done for you. (John 15:1-7)

Which scripture resonates with you? I suggest you find one to mediate on daily. Let the words of God saturate your spirit, so you can pour out to help your family and others in need. Remember the law of reciprocity. Sow good seeds, so you can reap a harvest of good fruit.

Use the space below to write your thoughts.

Heavenly Father,

Thank You for Your continual grace and mercy. I am so thankful that You have always been with me through my journey in life. I thank You for never leaving me nor forsaking me. Thank you for the next. Thank you for the new season. To everything there is a season and a time. Help me to discern the season and trust in Your timing. You have given me abundant life. You have given me purpose, so I trust in the plans that You have for me, to prosper me and not harm me, plans of a future and expected end. Continue to lead, guide and order my steps. Your word says to let our requests be known by prayer and supplication, so I intercede also for my husband and kids, that You direct their paths and strengthen them where they are weak. God, cover them and protect them every step of the way. I surrender my will and my plans so that Your will be done in our life. Thank You for being faithful even when we are not. Thank You for forgiveness of our sins by the blood of Jesus. Thank you in advance for answered prayers and victory in Jesus' name. Amen.

Grace Recipes

Turkey Apple Brie Panini with Honey Mustard Maple Mayonnaise

This fall inspired turkey apple brie panini with honey mustard maple mayo is the perfect sweet and savory combination.

yield: 1 SANDWICH

prep time: 5 minutes
cook time: 10 minutes
total time: 15 minutes

INGREDIENTS:

For sandwich:

- 2 slices multi grain bread
- 2 tablespoons unsalted butter
- 4 (1/2-inch-thick) slices Brie cheese
- 6 thin apple slices
- 1/4-pound sliced turkey
- 1/4 cup baby arugula

For mayo:

- 1/2 cup mayonnaise
- 2 tablespoons honey mustard
- 2 teaspoons pure maple syrup

DIRECTIONS:

For sandwich:

Preheat panini maker to medium heat.

Lay out bread and butter 1 side of each slices. Flip buttered sides over and spread on a thin layer of mayonnaise on each slices of bread. Continue make sandwich by layering on the following - 2 slices Brie cheese, 3 apple slices, turkey, baby arugula, apple slices, Brie cheese and other slice of bread - butter side out.

Add sandwich to panini maker and press for about 10 minutes until the turkey is hot and the cheese is melted. (optional)

Cut sandwich in half

Note: If you don't have a Panini maker, you can use a griddle or cast-iron skillet.

Fruit Salad

This Spring/Summer inspired recipe for Fruit Salad is the perfect side or light snack during your family backyard gatherings. Choose your flavored syrup and dressing and enjoy!

prep time: 5 minutes
cook time: 30 minutes
total time: 35 minutes

INGREDIENTS:
- 8 pints strawberries, hulled and halved
- 4 pints blueberries
- 4 pints blackberries
- 4 cups green grapes, halved
- 4 cups red grapes, halved
- Fresh mint leaves

DIRECTIONS:

Prep fruit and refrigerate to cool
Choose a flavored dressing by preparing one of the Syrups.
Take fruit from refrigerator and stir in desired flavor.
Serve immediately

Orange Vanilla Syrup

- 2 cup sugar
- Zest and juice of 2 orange
- 2 vanilla beans

Place the sugar, 1 cup water, orange zest, juice and vanilla bean in a small pan and stir to dissolve the sugar. Then bring to a boil. Turn the heat to low and simmer for about 15 minutes to thicken. Set aside to cool. Garnish with mint leaves

Lime & Basil Syrup

- 2 lime
- 2 tablespoon mild flavored honey
- 2 tablespoon chopped fresh basil

Zest the lime into a small bowl and set aside for later use. Juice the lime into a second small bowl and add the honey and chopped basil. Mix well and set aside. Garnish with lime zest over fruit.

Ginger Vanilla Syrup

- 2 cups water
- 2 cups granulated sugar
- 1-inch knob fresh ginger root, peeled and sliced into coin
- 4 teaspoons vanilla extract

In a small saucepan, combine the water, sugar, and ginger. Bring to a boil then lower the heat and let simmer for 10 minutes. Stir to make sure all the sugar dissolved. Remove the pan from the heat and stir in the vanilla extract. Let the mixture steep for 30 minutes. Strain into a clean bowl and let cool completely.

Chicken & Sausage Gumbo with Okra

This Winter inspired dish is comfort and joy in a bowl on a cold, cozy day. Gumbo is cooked in many different ways and it is served in almost every home in Louisiana.

INGREDIENTS:

- 3 pounds chicken (boneless skinless breast and thigh recommended) cut in pieces
- 20 ounces Andouille sausage cooked, sliced
- 1 cup olive oil
- 3 quarts water
- 3 quarts chicken stock
- 1 pounds cut okra, (frozen if fresh is not available) (Optional)
- 2 -1/2 cups canola oil
- 2 cups flour
- 2 -1/2 cups yellow onion diced
- 2 -1/2 cups bell pepper diced
- 2- ½ cups celery diced,
- 1 teaspoon cayenne pepper, or chili pepper (use less for lower spiciness)
- 2 teaspoons black pepper
- 1 teaspoon paprika
- 2 teaspoon garlic powder
- 2 teaspoons kosher salt
- 1 tablespoons gumbo file powder

DIRECTIONS:

Season chicken with spices and herbs.

In a medium sized skillet already heated and lightly coated with olive oil, add chicken breast and thighs and sauté. Remove once fully cooked.

In "Gumbo Pot" or stock pot, add canola oil, flour on low heat and whisk until roux is brown caramel in color. Be careful to constantly stir on low heat and don't burn the roux.

After roux is ready, add and sauté trinity (onions, bell peppers, celery) until onion is translucent. Add okra and cook for about 10 minutes. (Okra is optional)

Add chicken and sausage, stir and cook for another 10 minutes. Add stock and simmer for 30 minutes. Adjust flavoring as needed by adding more spices. You may add water depending on how thick you want the gumbo.

Turn the heat off and add gumbo file powder. Stir.

Serve over cooked rice.

Happy Cooking

&

Say Grace

www.ingramcontent.com/pod-product-compliance
Lightning Source LLC
Chambersburg PA
CBHW071414290426
44108CB00014B/1817